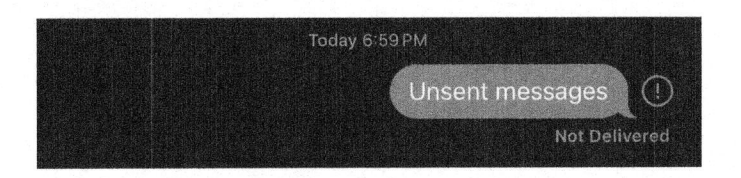

unsent messages

unsent messages

Copyright © 2025 by keith

independently published

ISBN: 9798308809081

all rights reserved

instagram.com/*keithpoetry_*
instagram.com/*unsentmessages_keithpoetry*

keith

why... does it feel like i have you
but sometimes
its like you're not even there...

unsent messages

why...does it feel like
i should have everything which i do..
since i have you but...
at the same time you feel so far away...

keith

why...does my heart hurt so much
right now...
i don't even know what to do...

unsent messages

why...am i crying alone
when i should have you by my side...

keith

why...can't you feel
that i am not by your side right now?

unsent messages

as i sit here on the couch at night
wanting to sleep
my body is yearning for you...

keith

i couldn't sleep without knowing
do you feel the same way about me now

unsent messages

the things you do
why does it not match the things
you say to me...

keith

i know i'm not perfect
but please don't leave me...

unsent messages

why is it so hard to tell you
how i really feel...

keith

i can't get you off my mind
do you even think about me even
for a second?

unsent messages

why am i so scared to loose you
when you're not even mine...

keith

i wish someday
i can be your priority

unsent messages

why am i so scared to loose you
when you don't even look my way

keith

i wish someday
you'll be able to receive these
unsent messages

unsent messages

why am i so scared to loose you
when you text other people
even when we are alone together

keith

i wish someday
you'll choose me first

unsent messages

i see you finally smile from far away
but sadly someone else
is making you smile

keith

i wish someday
you'll run to me when you
need a shoulder to cry on...

unsent messages

i hope you think about me
even for a second of you time when
you're with someone new

keith

i wish someday
you'll love me as much
as i love you...

unsent messages

i hope you know how much
i miss you right now

keith

i wish someday
all the hurt i'm feeling now
will turn to happiness

unsent messages

i hope you know how much
you mean to me

keith

i wish someday
you'll know how much
i have cried for you without you knowing

unsent messages

i hope you know how much
it hurts to see you with someone else
that could make you smile

keith

i wish someday
you'll miss me as much
as i miss you the second you leave
the room

unsent messages

i hope you know how much
it hurts after all these years seeing
you happy with someone else

keith

i wish someday
i would wake up beside you
for the rest of my life

unsent messages

i lost myself trying to find
our past memories on my phone

keith

i wish someday
i would be your first choice

unsent messages

i wish it was me
by your side as you
watch the sunset with someone else

keith

i wish someday
you'll be scared of loosing me too

unsent messages

i wish it was me
who you would send pictures
of beautiful sunsets

keith

i wish someday
you can't live a day without me too

unsent messages

i wish you knew the pain
i felt as i see you
sending a photo of the sunset we
both are looking at to someone else

keith

i wish someday
i'll be important enough for you
to put your phone down
when we are together

unsent messages

i wish i could be someone
you love in your life
even for a moment

keith

i wish someday
you can see how much
i love you

unsent messages

i wish i could be someone
that you would fall for
even for a moment of your life

keith

i wish someday
you'll come home to me

unsent messages

i wish i could be someone
that would make you smile
even for a moment

keith

would you ever see me
more than a friend?

unsent messages

you are the reason
i could not love anyone else

keith

you can break every part
of me but i would keep coming
back to you

unsent messages

you gave me the scars
but here i am wanting more of you

keith

you could tear me apart
so easily
but i will always choose you
than anyone else in this world

unsent messages

tear me apart into pecies
i would pick myself up and
run back to you

keith

i remember trying to follow
my brain
but my heart won and wants you
more than ever

unsent messages

why am i crying over a person
who sleeps well at night
not knowing i'm crying myself to sleep

keith

i should have hugged you
as tight as i could
before you slipped away from me

unsent messages

why would you waste your
time on me
when you knew you wouldn't stay
any longer...

keith

i should have kissed you
when i had a chance

unsent messages

i knew you didn't love me
as much as i love you
but why do i feel like you do?

keith

you were never mine
but why does it feel a half of me
died when you left me on seen?

unsent messages

is it too late to save
whatever we have?

keith

you told me you want to stay
as friends
i said yes...
but the pain being with you everyday
hurts more than dying

unsent messages

please don't let me go
i would stay forever even if you
do not want me too

keith

as i was with someone else
i was always wishing i was with you

unsent messages

please don't let me go
i would give you everything just
stay with me

keith

as i was with someone else
watching the stars
i wish it was you with me
as we gaze at the stars

unsent messages

why am i so scared of loosing you
as if you are my life line

keith

as i was with someone else
i realised i could never look at them
the same way i look at you

unsent messages

everyone around us sees
how much i love you
do you even notice
my love just a little bit?

keith

i gave everything of me
but you still choose someone
else over me

unsent messages

do you ever remember me
when you watch the sunset
with someone else?

keith

i gave you everything
but you still choose to tear me
into peices

unsent messages

is it too late to say how much
you mean to me?

keith

i hope one day you'll realise
my love for you was the only
real thing in thsi f*cked up world

unsent messages

i tried everything i could do
but you still left me behind
and move on to someone else

keith

i hope one day you'll realise
i was by your side when no one else
was

unsent messages

do you know the hardest part
of letting you go
is knowing that you were never
mine in the first place

keith

"maybe" something you
always tell me...
will we always be a maybe?

unsent messages

being by your side everyday
is the most painful feeling ever
but its also the best feeling ever

keith

do you know that your little
jokes about the past still hurts
as if a knife is being priced thru my
heart...

unsent messages

are you tired of me?
sometimes it feels like you're far
even though you are right by my side

keith

will you remember me?
will you remember the days that
i made you smile even for a second?

unsent messages

if i walk away right now...
will you even chase after me?

keith

as i look at my phone
here i am hoping your name
would come up and ask me how i am

unsent messages

you say you love me
but why are you running away
from me?

keith

will you ever regret
that you choose someone else
instead of choosing me?

unsent messages

i miss you but..
i couldn't send you a message
knowing you're already happy
with someone else

keith

you say you love me
but why do you keep pushing me
away?

unsent messages

without you right now
feels like i'm under the water
trying to swim out
but i keep drowning

keith

im drowning in my own
tears...
crying out your name that hurts my
tongue as i scream your name

unsent messages

do you even think of
sending me a message?

keith

have you moved on?
have you moved on to someone
someone who would love you
more than i did?

unsent messages

i don't think someone else would
love you as much as i do

keith

i haven't moved on
i still think about you every
single second...
i wonder if you ever think about me too

unsent messages

you were never mine
but why does it feel like we just
broke up all of a sudden?

keith

we were making jokes
about broken hearts
mine was not a joke
mine was shattered into pieces
as we laugh about our hearts being broken

unsent messages

learning that i broke your
heart
broke mine more and more
as if my heart just turned into dust

keith

you told me to love someone else
but all i ever wanted was to love you

unsent messages

i want to give you all my love
but now i can't since you're with
someone else that makes you happy

keith

the things you do..
why does it not match the things
you tell me?

unsent messages

i've been with someone else
but even then
they see that all i see is you while
looking at them in the eyes

keith

i may have held someone else
hand but all i wish was...
i wish it was you who's hand i was
holding on to

unsent messages

you are the one i want
can't you see that?
can't you see how much i love you?
the whole world sees it
but not you

keith

i'm i even holding on to something?
do we even have something to hold
on to?
is there even any strings attatched?

unsent messages

remember those times
when you said you would be with me?
when you said you would stay by my side?
where are you now?

keith

every night i wonder
do you think about me before you
sleep?

unsent messages

why does the night feel colder
now that you're not beside me anymore

keith

as tears fall form your eyes
i start to worry
i start to panic
can i do anything to stop those tears
falling form your eyes?

unsent messages

all i ever wanted is to see your smile again
but why do i see tears falling from
your eyes?

keith

am i even enough to make you
smile again?

unsent messages

rain is pouring today
i wonder if that was the tears
that continue to fall from last night...

keith

was i ever enough for you?

unsent messages

why does it feel that you're so
far away
as you lay next to me

keith

i may not be perfect
but i will try my best to be the
perfect one for you

unsent messages

can we watch the sun set
on last time before we say goodbye?

keith

i want to tell you everything
but i'm scared that you might just
leave me in an instant
if you knew that i want to be
more than just a friend

unsent messages

i want to keep whatever
relationship we have now
more than anything in this world
so please don't ever leave me

keith

am i even holding on to something?
am i even holding on to a thin string?
is there even anything to hold on?
or am i just imagining that there is
even a string to hold on to?

unsent messages

seeing you happy from a distance
is enough for me...
but it does leave a scar every time
i see you happy with someone else

keith

you say you love the attention
i'm giving you..
but what if one day someone else
would give you the same attention
i am giving you
will you leave me?

unsent messages

will the thought of you leaving me
will it ever disappear?
will it ever go away?
or will the pain just be there until the end?

keith

the hardest goodbye is the one that
you least unexpected
a goodbye where the other person
never heard you say it...

unsent messages

will you ever look my way
just once in your life
have you thought of being with me?

keith

who knew it was the last time
the last time i would see the smile
on your face
i should have captured the moment one
last time
before you were gone...

unsent messages

you never really said goodbye
but it feels like you'll be back
even though i know you wont
because it would be impossible..

keith

you were my whole world
but i was just a stranger you met
one day and just left...

unsent messages

the hardest goodbye is the one
you never saw it coming...

keith

who knew that the next day
we will both be just strangers
with memories of each other...

unsent messages

remember me?
we used to be together everyday
now we walk past each other as if
nothing happened between us...

keith

sometimes i have this urge
to just drive at the middle of the night
knock on your door...
hug you and tell you how much i miss you

unsent messages

in this crowd of people
all i see is you...

keith

all these noise that surrounds us
all i hear is your voice...

unsent messages

as tears fall from your eyes
i start to worry
i start to panic
can i do anything to wipe those tears
falling from your eyes

keith

all i wanted was to see was your smile again
all i can see is tears falling
am i even enough to make you
smile again?

unsent messages

the rain is pouring today
i wonder if that was the tears
to continue to pour from last night

keith

was i ever enough for you?

unsent messages

why does it feel that you're so far away
as you lay next to me

keith

i may not be perfect
but i will try my best to be the
perfect one for you

unsent messages

Its 11:29pm all i can say is i love you

keith

Waiting for you...
Waiting for you to love me back

unsent messages

Waiting for you to need me in your life

keith

Waiting for you...
Waiting for you to choose me

unsent messages

Will you ever choose me
to be with you?
Will you ever choose me
 to be with you for the rest of your life?

keith

I'll wait till my last breath
because you're the only one i want

unsent messages

I only want you no one else

keith

I want to be by your side
 till the last star falls from the sky

unsent messages

Will you ever look my way?

keith

Will you ever see me
as how i see you?

unsent messages

Will you ever look at me
the way i look at you?

keith

Will you ever love me
 as much as i love you?

unsent messages

Will i ever be enough for you
to choose me first?

keith

Will i ever be enough
to make you smile?

unsent messages

Its hard to watch you smile
from far away
but i guess that is the only way
for me to see you smile

keith

being away from you
made me think
are you geniunely happy
with the people around you?

unsent messages

follwing the last page...
or have you ever been genuinely happy
when you're with me?

keith

time can really be slow
without you with me

unsent messages

we have spent the last months
together everyday
no wonder i sit here and realise
life is not really fun without you anymore

keith

i got so used to being around you
everyday
that a day that goes without
feels like i am also slowly
dying inside

unsent messages

you became my comfort
on tough days
now that you're not with me
it feels like i don't know what step
to take next

keith

you told me to read a book
a book that you love
but here i am making a book instead
because i do not know where
to put my thought in

unsent messages

you say i don't miss you
or think about you
but here i am missing you
the day you left me
here i am thinking about you 24/7

keith

i couldn't really focus on anything else
so here i am typing my way out
through this book
for maybe some people would relate

unsent messages

it hurts me to think that
you are not with me now
but i know i have to move on
day by day

keith

they say the happiest people
from the outside
screams for help in the inside
and that is true here i am missing someone
so deeply that it hurts
but no one knows

unsent messages

you seem to keep your head
up high
while here i am looking down
and can't even face the truth

keith

do you ever think of me?
as you are away from me now?
do you miss me?

unsent messages

am i too late?
too late to say sorry for the mistakes
i have done

keith

is it too late to go back
how we used to be?
happy?

unsent messages

i know i told you i did a mistake
i knew it was a mistake
can you still forgive me?

keith

i feel so empty without you
beside me

unsent messages

please come back to me
i just cant live a world without you anymore

keith

can't you come back running
into my arms again?

unsent messages

without you
i don't feel like living anymore
you have become a part of me

keith

can you look at my way
like how you used to look at me
with happines filled in your eyes

unsent messages

all i see when you look at me
is emptiness in your eyes

keith

you don't look my way anymore
but i would still take a shot for you

unsent messages

if ever we cross paths again
will there be a spark?

keith

if ever we could turn back time
will we have done things differently?

unsent messages

will we have changed our past
so we do not fall out of love?

keith

remember those road trips we had?
felt like it was just a dream
i couldn't reach to anymore

unsent messages

remember when we use to watch
the stars by the beach at night
those were the happiest moments of my life

keith

remember those cafe's by work
as i pass by them
i just see you in every corner of it

unsent messages

maybe next time ill be enough for you

keith

maybe you'll be the one for me
if we ever change the past

unsent messages

i miss you so badly
i'm gasping for air

keith

will these unsent messages
ever reach you one day

unsent messages

will these unsent messages
be heard?

keith

will these unsent messages
will ever be sent to you?

unsent messages

i'm lying to myself everyday
that i can live without you

keith

the only reason i live
is because of your smile

unsent messages

please keep smiling even though
it hurts me
to see you with someone else

keith

please live the life you've always wanted
even when i'm not by your side

unsent messages

everyday as i wake up
a piece of me is falling apart
knowing that you're waking up
without me by your side

keith

if we have met in the right time
would our ending be different?

unsent messages

if we have met in the right place
will we even have a ending?

keith

i miss your voice

unsent messages

i miss waking up by your side

keith

i miss hugging you goodnight
till we both fall asleep

unsent messages

i can't even make my own morning coffee
as i used to make us coffee

keith

i can't even eat my favourite food
as it became our favourite food

unsent messages

i can't even walk the same streets
without seeing the memory of us

keith

i can't even stare at my own ceiling
as we were both looking at them
as if we could see the starts through it

unsent messages

people say time heals but it doesn't
the wounds are just covered
but it opens everytime
i think about you

keith

speaking of wounds
what i have now is a on going pain
as if there's just a knife pierced
in my heart all day long

unsent messages

you're worth every tear i have cried

keith

but sometimes i wonder what if
what if we never met?

unsent messages

what if we never held hands?

keith

what if our eyes didn't meet that day?

unsent messages

will i still have the pain
i'm feeling right now with someone else?

keith

will our paths still cross?

unsent messages

was i meant to have this
much pain in my life?

keith

everyday as i wake up
it feels like something is always missing
and i guess its waking up without you
by my side is the missing feeling i have

unsent messages

will we always just be a dream
that i used to have?

keith

will these unsent messages
ever be read by you?

unsent messages

will these unsent messages
ever see the light? or will it forever
be hidden in the dark?

keith

was our love ever true?
or was it always a lie?

unsent messages

was our love not enough
that you have to go and look for love
with someone else?

keith

my life has been black and white
since you walked out of my life

unsent messages

was our love honest?
or was everything all a lie that
we called love?

keith

i never thought we would just
be a memory

unsent messages

all of these unsent messages
i write them to you hoping my phone
would just glitch with a mind of its own
and send them all to you for you to read
and know what i feel right now
without you by my side
but i guess my phone would not do that
so i'm writing it all down in this book
hoping one day it will reach you...

keith

these unsent messages
will be over after this page
i know these messages will never be sent
but i hope you are doing well
thank you for inspiring me to write my feelings
into a book which you would not really know
for the readers of this book
i just want to say you are not alone
heart breaks can be in any form

from losing anyone you love from your
grandparents, parents, brother, sister, friends,
love ones. this book is messages hope to reach
them where ever they might be in this world.

if you have reached the ending of this book.
i *Keith* thank you from the bottom of my heart
and remind you that YOU ARE NOT ALONE.

Thank you,

Keith
unsent messages

Printed in Great Britain
by Amazon